THE BALDIE GIRL'S JOURNAL TO FREEDOM

A BALDIE BOOK

THE BALDIE GIRL'S JOURNAL TO FREEDOM

ONLY YOU CAN TELL YOUR STORY

By Shelia Marie Hunter

This book belongs to:

I dedicate this book, first, to the three who created me – God, Carrie Louise Hunter, and Horace Herman Hunter, my parents. Thanks for preparing me to handle life's lessons.

To my husband James and daughter Erica, you are my life and everything that is good. Thanks for being my support system and always letting me know that I am so much more than the hair I no longer have. You have allowed me to be vulnerable while discovering my strength within.

To my brother Clarence, thanks for helping me bring one of my many dreams to life. Brothers are forever.

To every woman concealing her true self, remember that we were born to be confidently great. Embrace your Boldness, your Baldness, and your Beauty as you step out into the world.

PREFACE

I have enjoyed being a hairstylist for 35 years. My interest in cosmetology started early on after my hair began to thin in my Junior year in high school. I was later diagnosed with alopecia. Alopecia is a hair loss disorder that affects millions worldwide. To cover my hair loss, I began using hair extensions. The extensions bolstered my confidence and sparked a desire to help others who suffered from hair disorders. At this pivotal moment in my life, I fell in love with the idea of enhancing the beauty and confidence of others through hair styling. After officially launching my career in 1990, I quickly became skilled in hair weaving and wig-making for my clients and myself.

My education, training, and early success in haircare and makeup led to me becoming one of the top 30 stylists in Atlanta, selected to provide beauty services for athletes and officials during the 1996 Olympic Games. Later, in 2000, I moved to Dallas and opened Studio 957, my first salon in 2004. My vision for the salon made me one of the most sought-after stylists in the Dallas high-profile community.

Despite my professional success, I still struggled internally with my hair loss. Having been diagnosed with alopecia at an early age, I learned to navigate the silent struggles of hair loss while being a mother, wife, and caregiver to my 103-year-old father. Remembering one of the early and most devastating days in my journey, the last patch of hair that made me feel normal was now gone. I no longer had enough hair on top to cover my weave in the front.

Early in our marriage, my husband assured me he was okay with me shaving my remaining hair. My daughter, age six then, wasn't ready for anyone to know her mother was bald. The shame that comes with hair loss affects the entire family. Little did I know that nearly 12 years later, on the morning of March 28, 2018, my daughter would finally be okay with me being bald. It would be my last day in hiding. Never would I cover my Beautiful Crown again. I felt both naked and free, though unsure of what others would think. I've been living So Free Since and loving it.

I created this journal as a therapeutic outlet, offering a space for women like myself to process their journey from loss to acceptance and freedom. Here, you can tell your story in your own words and at your own pace.

ABOUT THIS JOURNAL

The goal of this journal is to be a source of empowerment, inspiration, and a guide for those overcome by hair loss to emerge stronger.
The journal exercises will assist you in navigating through all the pain and daily struggles – and, if it is the case, choosing to shave your head.

As you start to journal your hair loss, turn each month to Chapter 7 - Caring For Me, and use the five worksheets designed to help you establish healthy self-care practices. Revisit the worksheets for each month to do the exercises.

CHAPTER 1: MY BALDIE TRUTH – outlines the start of your journey – allowing you to reflect on the initial signs of hair loss and an opportunity to share emotions and circumstances that follow.

CHAPTER 2: THE PATH AHEAD – assists you in navigating the stages of grief upon receiving your diagnosis. You are guided through facing the emotions that accompany your new truth.

CHAPTER 3: MY DECISION TO LIVE FREE – explores the smooth but naked truth of hair loss and embraces the challenges of adapting to a new reality that can be hard. Acceptance is a powerful thing.

CHAPTER 4: LOVE AND INTIMACY BALD – is about accepting the new you and learning to love and be loved on your terms.

CHAPTER 5: SO FREE FROM – celebrates freedom and release from shame and bondage while learning to care less about people's perceptions and embracing your authentic self.

CHAPTER 6: SINCE BECOMING SO FREE – embarks on the self- acceptance and positive changes that come with putting secrecy and hiding in the rear view. You can tell your story.

CHAPTER 7: CARING FOR ME – uses five monthly worksheets, to prioritize Healthy Habits and Self-Care Rituals, while recognizing that your health is your greatest asset.

CHAPTER 8: THE BALDIE PLAN – sets forth a path of pursuing your dreams with great confidence while reclaiming your identity and envisioning a future of limitless potential.

CHAPTER 9: THE BALDIE LAWS – suggest rules to live by and to guide you in your new life of freedom. These rules will shine light on your path and offer strength and guideposts as you continue your journey.

CONTENTS

12 CHAPTER 1
MY BALDIE TRUTH

14 Disbelief

16 Self Diagnosis

18 Share or Silence

20 Anger

22 Finding Cover

24 Physician Diagnosis

28 CHAPTER 2
THE PATH AHEAD

30 Navigating Grief

32 Cry for Help

34 My Safe Place

36 Confronting Fear

38 Acceptance

40 My Choices

44 CHAPTER 3
MY DECISION TO LIVE FREE

46 The Struggles

48 The Defining Moment

50 All Those Questions

52 Workplace Anxiety

54 Finding Liberation

56 Emerging Confidence

60 CHAPTER 4
LOVE AND INTIMACY BALD

62 Dreaming of Intimacy

64 Seeing Yourself Through Their Eyes

66 Vulnerability

68 Confidence in Lingerie

70 Opening Up

72 Touch of Affection

76 CHAPTER 5
SO FREE FROM

78 Releasing Shame

80 Embracing Freedom

82 Challenging Ignorance

84 Conquering Insecurities

86 Letting Go of Blame

88 Seeking Validation

92 CHAPTER 6
SINCE BECOMING SO FREE

94 Expressing Your Style

96 Reflecting in the Mirror

98 Envisioning Your Future

100 Embracing Your True Self

102 Supporting Others on Their Journey

104 Embracing Emotions

108 CHAPTER 7
CARING FOR ME

110 Monthly Reflection

111 Monthly Self-Assessment

112 Affirming My Values

113 Self-Care In Practice

114 Monthly Water Challenge

140 52-Weeks Weight Tracker

142 CHAPTER 8
MY BALDIE PLAN

144 My Baldie Bucket List

146 Yearly Vision Planner

148 My Goals and Dreams

150 Letters to Myself

158 CHAPTER 9
MY BALDIE LAWS

174 REFLECTIONS

1
MY BALDIE TRUTH

As you begin your journey, you will find yourself reflecting on the subtle signs of hair loss. The thinning patches, receding hairline, and strands in your brush all hint at a change you can no longer ignore. The emotions swirl within you – the denial and frustration hit you as you come face-to-face with the reality staring back from the mirror. The circumstances surrounding the onset of your hair loss weigh heavily on your mind, leaving you questioning why it's happening and what it means for your identity and self-image.

With each strand lost, you feel the weight of life changes – physical and emotional. Am I ignoring my shedding hair everywhere.

These moments become the foundation of your journey, propelling you on a path of self-discovery and growth as you confront the baldie truth head-on.

DISBELIEF

Date ....

Am I ignoring my shedding hair everywhere? Strands in my comb and brush, in my sink, and patches are developing on my head. Share your story of this initial trauma.

....

....

....

....

....

....

....

....

....

....

....

....

One takeaway I must remember...

SELF-DIAGNOSIS

Date ....

Can these vitamins, home remedies, and oils work for me? I need a miracle. Let me check on YouTube or WebMD for some answers. There must be answers somewhere. Share a similar story of your search for solutions.

....

....

....

....

....

....

....

....

....

....

....

....

....

....

....

....

....

....

One takeaway I must remember...

SHARE OR SILENCE

Date ....

I am not sure what is happening with my hair. This problem has been going on too long, and I am getting scared. Several of my girlfriends are wearing weaves. Should I ask them if they are experiencing the same problem? Tell your story and what you decided.

....

....

....

....

....

....

....

....

....

....

....

....

....

One takeaway I must remember...

ANGER

Date ....

I do not know what to do. I feel overwhelmed and want to lash out; my frustration and anger are eating away at me, and I have never felt so upset. I want to know why I am losing all my hair. Talk about your feelings of anger and how you reacted.

....

....

....

....

....

....

....

....

....

....

....

....

....

....

....

....

....

....

....

....

....

....

....

One takeaway I must remember...

....

....

....

FINDING COVER

Date ....

When will I know if what's happening is real or not? I know my hair is falling out, but is it temporary or forever? How will I face my family, friends and co-workers? It's time to confront my reality – should I wear wigs, weaves, or hats? Tell your story of a similar dilemma.

....

....

....

....

....

....

....

....

....

....

....

....

....

....

....

....

One takeaway I must remember...

PHYSICIAN DIAGNOSES

Date ....

Finally, I see the doctor, hoping to get answers to calm my mind. I cannot go on without knowing what is happening to me. Is it possible that I have Alopecia, Lupus, Cancer, or some other condition? What is your story?

....

....

....

....

....

....

....

....

....

....

....

....

....

....

One takeaway I must remember...

FREE THOUGHTS

2
THE PATH AHEAD

The path ahead involves navigating the stages of grief after receiving your diagnosis and facing many emotions. Denial is the first hurdle as you struggle to accept your new reality. You may question the validity of your diagnosis or hope that it's all just a temporary setback.

As denial begins to fade, anger may take its place, directed inwardly at yourself or outwardly at your circumstances. You may resent your body, feeling it has betrayed you, or the world, feeling it has been unfair. Acceptance eventually finds its place deep within – bringing a sense of peace and a newfound understanding of your journey ahead.

NAVIGATING GRIEF

Date ....

The diagnosis is definite, and I now know what's going on. However, I am struggling with deep feelings of sadness and depression that I have never experienced. At times, I find myself crying inwardly and wanting to scream. Grief happens in many ways – telling your story can offer some relief.

....

....

....

....

....

....

....

....

....

....

....

....

....

....

CRY FOR HELP

Date ....

How long can I continue hiding this secret? I don't feel like telling anyone or going to work. My life is a hidden mess. I am dying inside, and I want to run away. Tell your story of wanting to cry out for help but not knowing how.

....

....

....

....

....

....

....

....

....

....

....

....

....

One takeaway I must remember...

MY SAFE PLACE

Date ....

The world is closing in on me, and I desperately need a place to share whats going on with me. I know my family should be a soft place if I need to let go, but can I count on them for strength and support. They love me and I hope they understand my feelings. Share your story of who became your safe place of refuge.

....

....

....

....

....

....

....

....

....

....

....

....

....

....

....

One takeaway I must remember...

CONFRONTING FEAR

Date ....

I am unsure whether to keep my hair with its patches or go ahead and shave it all off. I may have bumps or lumps in my head or an unflattering shape. I don't know how I may look without hair or even want to imagine being bald. Share your fears and concerns about shaving your head.

....

....

....

....

....

....

....

....

....

....

....

....

....

....

One takeaway I must remember...

ACCEPTANCE

Date ....

Now that I know my truth, I can either reject the truth I have learned or gracefully embrace whatever is ahead of me with dignity and self-love. I am not my hair, and freedom comes when acceptance begins. Tell your story of starting to embrace your new life.

....

....

....

....

....

....

....

....

....

....

....

....

....

....

One takeaway I must remember...

MY CHOICES

Date ....

I don't know whether I should continue using protective styles or go bald. Some of the wigs and weaves I have seen are attractive. Although I know that whatever I choose is my choice, I want to make a choice that will make me happy and boost my self confidence. Share how you managed your choices.

....

....

....

....

....

....

....

....

....

....

....

....

....

....

One takeaway I must remember...

FREE THOUGHTS

3
MY DECISION TO LIVE FREE

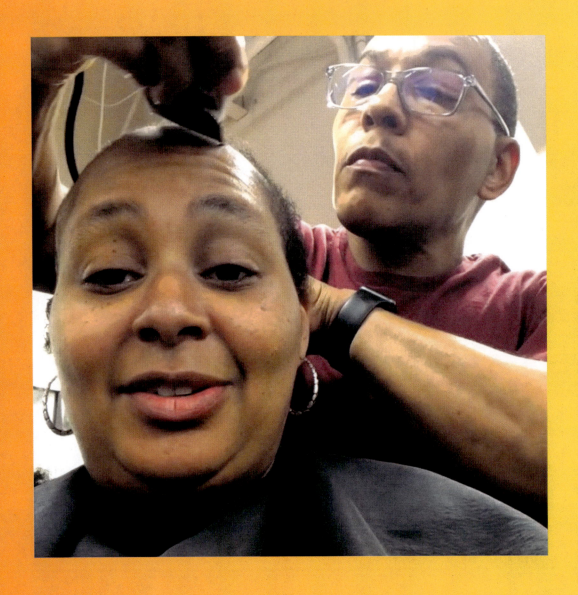

In this chapter, you delve into the truth of your hair loss and how you will manage it. You come to know that there is no one-size-fits-all solution to freedom. Whether you opt for wigs, weaves, wraps, or baldness, the choice is all yours. It is crucial to embrace whatever challenges emerge from adapting to your new reality, as acceptance promises immense power.

As you continue your hair loss journey, remember it's a personal experience. Each option you consider has its own set of benefits and perhaps drawbacks. Embrace the empowerment of making your own choice and accepting your unique path.

Walking in the freedom you choose, your Boldness, Baldness, and Beauty are not just qualities but are statements of Self-love and Acceptance – the place where freedom begins.

THE STRUGGLES

Date ....

The hardest thing about my hair loss has been dealing with deep feelings of emotional pain. I feel like I have lost part of me. And there are the feelings of no longer being attractive, not wanting to go outside, and everyone's staring. Share your struggles.

....

....

....

....

....

....

....

....

....

....

....

....

....

....

One takeaway I must remember...

THE DEFINING MOMENT

Date ....

There is no one-size-fits-all solution in deciding to be free. Your choice of wigs, weaves, hats, or shaving your head bald is ultimately your choice alone. For those who choose bald, as your freedom choice, this is your defining moment. Tell your story and decision of choosing to shave it all off and be free.

....

....

....

....

....

....

....

....

....

....

....

....

....

....

....

....

....

One takeaway I must remember...

ALL THOSE QUESTIONS

Date ....

Frequently, I get personal questions about my bald head from people I know and even strangers. Maybe once my scalp is no longer blotchy and all one tone, the questions will stop. Describe what it was like for you.

....

....

....

....

....

....

....

....

....

....

....

....

....

....

One takeaway I must remember...

WORKPLACE ANXIETY

Date ....

Co-workers are making assumptions about my shaved head and think that maybe they should feel sorry for me. I imagine some even wonder if it will impact my performance. If you can relate, share your story.

....

....

....

....

....

....

....

....

....

....

....

....

....

One takeaway I must remember...

FINDING LIBERATION

Date ....

Who would have thought that a shaved head could be so liberating? This new look has transformed my perspective on beauty and self-love. Share your feelings of being liberated when you finally embraced your baldness.

....

....

....

....

....

....

....

....

....

....

....

....

....

....

....

One takeaway I must remember...

EMERGING CONFIDENCE

Date ....

Embracing my baldness feels like a symbol of empowerment – the new me! Since becoming bald, I feel sexier than ever – even more so than when I had my hair. Tell the story of your emerging confidence and the changes you see.

....

....

....

....

....

....

....

....

....

....

....

....

....

....

One takeaway I must remember...

FREE THOUGHTS

4
LOVE AND INTIMACY BALD

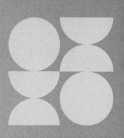

In "Love and Intimacy Bald," it's time to embrace the new you and learn to love and accept love on your terms. You'll steer through the complexities of relationships and self-worth in a world that often prioritizes physical appearance over inner beauty.

As you journal on this topic, contemplate the depths of intimacy and understand that authentic connection goes beyond the external. Embrace vulnerability as the foundation of a meaningful relationship as you discover the courage to let love in and cultivate relationships founded on mutual respect and understanding.

DREAMING OF INTIMACY

Date ....

I imagine that love and intimate situations as a bald woman will present a whole new and unique experience. Envision your ideal situations involving love and intimacy as a bald woman, and compare it to your current reality.

....

....

....

....

....

....

....

....

....

....

....

....

....

One takeaway I must remember...

SEEING YOURSELF THROUGH THEIR EYES

Date ....

You may perceive yourself somewhat differently now that you are bald and may also wonder how your partner perceives you. Reflect on how you imagine your partner's perception of you may have changed since shaving your head and how you perceive yourself in intimate moments.

....

....

....

....

....

....

....

....

....

....

....

....

....

....

....

....

....

....

One takeaway I must remember...

VULNERABILITY

Date ....

Now that you're bald, you may feel a greater sense of vulnerability or fearlessness, being naked from head to toe. Reflect on any insecurities or inhibitions you may have had before shaving your head and how you are coping with them now.

....

....

....

....

....

....

....

....

....

....

....

....

....

....

....

One takeaway I must remember...

CONFIDENCE IN LINGERIE

Date ....

Planning and setting the mood for a romantic evening brings a certain excitement. Has your sensual awareness and confidence in lingerie changed since becoming bald? Reflect on and share the complex feelings of awkwardness or boldness you experience when wearing lingerie.

....

....

....

....

....

....

....

....

....

....

....

....

....

....

One takeaway I must remember...

OPENING UP

Date ....

When deciding to shave my head, I knew I should share this decision with my partner. I believed that openness and honesty would be the best approach for our relationship and my peace of mind. Tell of your opening up and how it affected your relationship.

....

....

....

....

....

....

....

....

....

....

....

....

....

....

One takeaway I must remember...

TOUCH OF AFFECTION

Date ....

A gentle touch or caress of one's head is a more personal and intimate gesture than most people imagine. It can evoke strong emotions. Reflect on the first intimate moment when your partner touched your shaved head and how it made you feel.

....

....

....

....

....

....

....

....

....

....

....

....

....

....

....

One takeaway I must remember...

FREE THOUGHTS

5
SO FREE FROM

Here, you'll embark on a journey of celebration and liberation. It is time to cast off the shackles of shame and societal expectations and wholeheartedly embrace your authentic self with open arms.

On this part of your journey, you'll identify what you are leaving behind — including the doubts and criticisms that have made you question your beauty. In these pages, learn to care less about other's perceptions and enjoy the beauty of openness, vulnerability, and your uniqueness. Discover the strength and empowerment that emerges from being honest and truthful to yourself.

RELEASING SHAME

Date ....

Write about how you confronted and released the shame surrounding your hair loss, freeing yourself from its burden.

....

....

....

....

....

....

....

....

....

....

....

....

....

One takeaway I must remember...

EMBRACING FREEDOM

Date ....

Reflect on how you handled the rejection by others of your choice to be bald and embraced it confidently.

....

....

....

....

....

....

....

....

....

....

....

....

....

One takeaway I must remember...

CHALLENGING IGNORANCE

Date ....

Describe the moments when you faced ignorance and reactions from others and how you responded with strength and understanding.

....

....

....

....

....

....

....

....

....

....

....

One takeaway I must remember...

CONQUERING INSECURITIES

Date ....

While embracing your baldness, explore the insecurities you faced and the steps you took to overcome them and gain confidence.

....

....

....

....

....

....

....

....

....

....

....

....

....

....

One takeaway I must remember...

LETTING GO OF BLAME

Date ....

Reflect on how you stopped blaming yourself or others for things out of your control, including your hair loss, and eventually found peace within yourself.

....

....

....

....

....

....

....

....

....

....

....

....

....

....

One takeaway I must remember...

SEEKING VALIDATION

Date ....

Reflect on your journey of going outside without covering your head and the need for validation you may have once felt. Describe how you've learned to validate yourself.

....

....

....

....

....

....

....

....

....

....

....

....

....

....

....

....

....

....

....

....

....

....

....

....

....

....

....

One takeaway I must remember...

....

....

....

FREE THOUGHTS

6
SINCE BECOMING SO FREE

In this chapter, welcome to your journey of self-acceptance and positive change. Having left secrecy and hiding in the rearview, you can now embrace the confidence and power of your new reality. Step into your new truth unapologetically.

By engaging in self-reflection and emotional growth, you will discover your greatness as you embrace your true self. It's about living life authentically, without the constraints of fear, shame, and pretense. So, embark on the journey of becoming the best version of yourself, liberated and unafraid to shine.

EXPRESSING YOUR STYLE

Date ....

Now that you don't have to worry about your hair, share how your fashion choices reflect your personality and style.

....

....

....

....

....

....

....

....

....

....

....

....

....

....

One takeaway I must remember...

REFLECTING IN THE MIRROR

Date ....

Write about that very moment, since becoming free, when
you looked in the mirror and realized that you were enough.

....

....

....

....

....

....

....

....

....

....

....

....

....

....

....

....

....

....

....

....

....

....

....

....

One takeaway I must remember...

....

....

....

ENVISIONING YOUR FUTURE

Date ....

Now that you have embraced your baldness and found freedom, describe your dreams and aspirations for the future.

....

....

....

....

....

....

....

....

....

....

....

....

One takeaway I must remember...

EMBRACING YOUR TRUE SELF

Date ....

Reflect on how your confidence and boldness has grown as you've embraced the change in you and accepted yourself fully.

....

....

....

....

....

....

....

....

....

....

....

....

One takeaway I must remember...

....

....

....

SUPPORTING OTHERS ON THEIR JOURNEY

Date ....

Write about how you support and encourage others going through similar experiences with hair loss or self-acceptance.

....

....

....

....

....

....

....

....

....

....

....

....

One takeaway I must remember...

EMBRACING EMOTIONS

Date ....

Describe the emotions you feel now that you've found freedom and acceptance in being bald and how it has transformed your perspective on life.

....

....

....

....

....

....

....

....

....

....

....

....

....

One takeaway I must remember...

FREE THOUGHTS

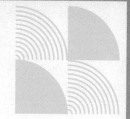

7

CARING FOR ME

This chapter highlights the importance of prioritizing healthy habits and self-care practices to nurture oneself. From skincare routines to mental health practices, you will recognize that your health is your greatest asset.

Discover, as you journal, the various self-care techniques tailored to your needs, cultivating a greater sense of well-being and resilience. Prioritize your physical, emotional, and mental health as you embark on this journey of caring for yourself. In the following monthly worksheets, discover the transformative and the emotional healing power of self-care.

MONTHLY REFLECTIONS

Reflect on your month by acknowledging your wins, addressing challenges, and extracting valuable lessons. Explore how these experiences make you feel and try to capture the essence of the month with one word.

MONTHLY WINS:

....

....

HOW DO YOUR WINS MAKE ME FEEL?

....

....

CHALLENGES:

....

....

HOW CAN I IMPROVE IT?

....

....

TWO LIFE LESSONS I LEARNED THIS MONTH:

....

....

ONE WORD THAT DESCRIBES THIS MONTH:

....

MONTHLY SELF-ASSESSMENT

Use this self-assessment worksheet to evaluate your physical, social, mental, and spiritual well-being. Reflect on your current practices and identify areas for improvement to enhance your overall wellness.

PHYSICAL SELF CARE

	Y	N
Got enough sleep	O	O
Eat healthy	O	O
Balanced diet	O	O
Get regular exercise	O	O
See a healthcare provider when needed	O	O

Note:

MENTAL SELF CARE

	Y	N
Take time to relax	O	O
Joy and fulfillment in activities	O	O
Support system	O	O
Practice mindfulness	O	O
Stay present in the moment	O	O

Note:

SOCIAL SELF CARE

	Y	N
Strong and supportive relationship with friends and family	O	O
Make time for social activity	O	O
Set boundaries	O	O
Say no when necessary	O	O

Note:

SPIRITUAL SELF CARE

	Y	N
Have a sense of purpose and meaning in your life	O	O
Practice self-reflection and mindfulness	O	O
Have a sense of connection to something larger than yourself	O	O

Note:

AFFIRMING MY VALUES

This worksheet will help you clarify your values and priorities by affirming what you are, what you are not, what you will, what you will not, what you can do, what you cannot do, what you want, and what you do not want, in your life.

I AM:	I AM NOT:
I WILL:	**I WILL NOT:**
I CAN:	**I CANNOT:**
I WANT:	**I DO NOT WANT:**

SELF-CARE IN PRACTICE

Explore and enhance your self-care routine with this worksheet. Reflect on relaxation practices, food choices, physical activity, personal connections, and spirituality. Identify any difficulties you may face in these areas. This worksheet will help you prioritize your well-being and develop strategies to overcome challenges.

RELAXATION PRACTICE	DIFFICULT FOR ME
FOOD CHOICES	DIFFICULT FOR ME
PHYSICAL ACTIVITY	DIFFICULT FOR ME
CONNECTION/SPIRITUALITY	DIFFICULT FOR ME

WATER CHALLENGE

Track your hydration and prioritize your health with this monthly water challenge worksheet. Set your goals, monitor your progress, and stay hydrated to feel your best every day.

GOAL

DAY 1   DAY 2   DAY 3   DAY 4

DAY 5   DAY 6   DAY 7   DAY 8

DAY 9   DAY 10   DAY 11   DAY 12

DAY 13   DAY 14   DAY 15   DAY 16

DAY 17   DAY 18   DAY 19   DAY 20

DAY 21   DAY 22   DAY 23   DAY 24

DAY 25   DAY 26   DAY 26   DAY 28

DAY 29   DAY 30   DAY 31

MONTHLY REFLECTIONS

Reflect on your month by acknowledging your wins, addressing challenges, and extracting valuable lessons. Explore how these experiences make you feel and try to capture the essence of the month with one word.

MONTHLY WINS:

....

....

HOW DO YOUR WINS MAKE ME FEEL?

....

....

CHALLENGES:

....

....

HOW CAN I IMPROVE IT?

....

....

TWO LIFE LESSONS I LEARNED THIS MONTH:

....

....

ONE WORD THAT DESCRIBES THIS MONTH:

....

MONTHLY SELF-ASSESSMENT

Use this self-assessment worksheet to evaluate your physical, social, mental, and spiritual well-being. Reflect on your current practices and identify areas for improvement to enhance your overall wellness.

PHYSICAL SELF CARE

	Y	N
Got enough sleep	O	O
Eat healthy	O	O
Balanced diet	O	O
Get regular exercise	O	O
See a healthcare provider when needed	O	O

Note:

MENTAL SELF CARE

	Y	N
Take time to relax	O	O
Joy and fulfillment in activities	O	O
Support system	O	O
Practice mindfulness	O	O
Stay present in the moment	O	O

Note:

SOCIAL SELF CARE

	Y	N
Strong and supportive relationship with friends and family	O	O
Make time for social activity	O	O
Set boundaries	O	O
Say no when necessary	O	O

Note:

SPIRITUAL SELF CARE

	Y	N
Have a sense of purpose and meaning in your life	O	O
Practice self-reflection and mindfulness	O	O
Have a sense of connection to something larger than yourself	O	O

Note:

AFFIRMING MY VALUES

This worksheet will help you clarify your values and priorities by affirming what you are, what you are not, what you will, what you will not, what you can do, what you cannot do, what you want, and what you do not want, in your life.

I AM:	I AM NOT:
I WILL:	**I WILL NOT:**
I CAN:	**I CANNOT:**
I WANT:	**I DO NOT WANT:**

SELF-CARE IN PRACTICE

Explore and enhance your self-care routine with this worksheet. Reflect on relaxation practices, food choices, physical activity, personal connections, and spirituality. Identify any difficulties you may face in these areas. This worksheet will help you prioritize your well-being and develop strategies to overcome challenges.

RELAXATION PRACTICE	DIFFICULT FOR ME
FOOD CHOICES	DIFFICULT FOR ME
PHYSICAL ACTIVITY	DIFFICULT FOR ME
CONNECTION/SPIRITUALITY	DIFFICULT FOR ME

WATER CHALLENGE

Track your hydration and prioritize your health with this monthly water challenge worksheet. Set your goals, monitor your progress, and stay hydrated to feel your best every day.

GOAL

DAY 1   DAY 2   DAY 3   DAY 4

DAY 5   DAY 6   DAY 7   DAY 8

DAY 9   DAY 10   DAY 11   DAY 12

DAY 13   DAY 14   DAY 15   DAY 16

DAY 17   DAY 18   DAY 19   DAY 20

DAY 21   DAY 22   DAY 23   DAY 24

DAY 25   DAY 26   DAY 26   DAY 28

DAY 29   DAY 30   DAY 31

MONTHLY REFLECTIONS

Reflect on your month by acknowledging your wins, addressing challenges, and extracting valuable lessons. Explore how these experiences make you feel and try to capture the essence of the month with one word.

MONTHLY WINS:

....

....

HOW DO YOUR WINS MAKE ME FEEL?

....

....

CHALLENGES:

....

....

HOW CAN I IMPROVE IT?

....

....

TWO LIFE LESSONS I LEARNED THIS MONTH:

....

....

ONE WORD THAT DESCRIBES THIS MONTH:

....

MONTHLY SELF-ASSESSMENT

Use this self-assessment worksheet to evaluate your physical, social, mental, and spiritual well-being. Reflect on your current practices and identify areas for improvement to enhance your overall wellness.

PHYSICAL SELF CARE

	Y	N
Got enough sleep	O	O
Eat healthy	O	O
Balanced diet	O	O
Get regular exercise	O	O
See a healthcare provider when needed	O	O

Note:

MENTAL SELF CARE

	Y	N
Take time to relax	O	O
Joy and fulfillment in activities	O	O
Support system	O	O
Practice mindfulness	O	O
Stay present in the moment	O	O

Note:

SOCIAL SELF CARE

	Y	N
Strong and supportive relationship with friends and family	O	O
Make time for social activity	O	O
Set boundaries	O	O
Say no when necessary	O	O

Note:

SPIRITUAL SELF CARE

	Y	N
Have a sense of purpose and meaning in your life	O	O
Practice self-reflection and mindfulness	O	O
Have a sense of connection to something larger than yourself	O	O

Note:

AFFIRMING MY VALUES

This worksheet will help you clarify your values and priorities by affirming what you are, what you are not, what you will, what you will not, what you can do, what you cannot do, what you want, and what you do not want, in your life.

I AM:	I AM NOT:
I WILL:	**I WILL NOT:**
I CAN:	**I CANNOT:**
I WANT:	**I DO NOT WANT:**

SELF-CARE IN PRACTICE

Explore and enhance your self-care routine with this worksheet. Reflect on relaxation practices, food choices, physical activity, personal connections, and spirituality. Identify any difficulties you may face in these areas. This worksheet will help you prioritize your well-being and develop strategies to overcome challenges.

RELAXATION PRACTICE	DIFFICULT FOR ME
FOOD CHOICES	DIFFICULT FOR ME
PHYSICAL ACTIVITY	DIFFICULT FOR ME
CONNECTION/SPIRITUALITY	DIFFICULT FOR ME

WATER CHALLENGE

Track your hydration and prioritize your health with this monthly water challenge worksheet. Set your goals, monitor your progress, and stay hydrated to feel your best every day.

GOAL

DAY 1
DAY 2
DAY 3
DAY 4

DAY 5
DAY 6
DAY 7
DAY 8

DAY 9
DAY 10
DAY 11
DAY 12

DAY 13
DAY 14
DAY 15
DAY 16

DAY 17
DAY 18
DAY 19
DAY 20

DAY 21
DAY 22
DAY 23
DAY 24

DAY 25
DAY 26
DAY 26
DAY 28

DAY 29
DAY 30
DAY 31

MONTHLY REFLECTIONS

Reflect on your month by acknowledging your wins, addressing challenges, and extracting valuable lessons. Explore how these experiences make you feel and try to capture the essence of the month with one word.

MONTHLY WINS:

....

....

HOW DO YOUR WINS MAKE ME FEEL?

....

....

CHALLENGES:

....

....

HOW CAN I IMPROVE IT?

....

....

TWO LIFE LESSONS I LEARNED THIS MONTH:

....

....

ONE WORD THAT DESCRIBES THIS MONTH:

....

MONTHLY SELF-ASSESSMENT

Use this self-assessment worksheet to evaluate your physical, social, mental, and spiritual well-being. Reflect on your current practices and identify areas for improvement to enhance your overall wellness.

PHYSICAL SELF CARE

	Y	N
Got enough sleep	O	O
Eat healthy	O	O
Balanced diet	O	O
Get regular exercise	O	O
See a healthcare provider when needed	O	O

Note:

MENTAL SELF CARE

	Y	N
Take time to relax	O	O
Joy and fulfillment in activities	O	O
Support system	O	O
Practice mindfulness	O	O
Stay present in the moment	O	O

Note:

SOCIAL SELF CARE

	Y	N
Strong and supportive relationship with friends and family	O	O
Make time for social activity	O	O
Set boundaries	O	O
Say no when necessary	O	O

Note:

SPIRITUAL SELF CARE

	Y	N
Have a sense of purpose and meaning in your life	O	O
Practice self-reflection and mindfulness	O	O
Have a sense of connection to something larger than yourself	O	O

Note:

AFFIRMING MY VALUES

This worksheet will help you clarify your values and priorities by affirming what you are, what you are not, what you will, what you will not, what you can do, what you cannot do, what you want, and what you do not want, in your life.

I AM:	I AM NOT:
I WILL:	I WILL NOT:
I CAN:	I CANNOT:
I WANT:	I DO NOT WANT:

SELF-CARE IN PRACTICE

Explore and enhance your self-care routine with this worksheet. Reflect on relaxation practices, food choices, physical activity, personal connections, and spirituality. Identify any difficulties you may face in these areas. This worksheet will help you prioritize your well-being and develop strategies to overcome challenges.

RELAXATION PRACTICE	DIFFICULT FOR ME
FOOD CHOICES	DIFFICULT FOR ME
PHYSICAL ACTIVITY	DIFFICULT FOR ME
CONNECTION/SPIRITUALITY	DIFFICULT FOR ME

WATER CHALLENGE

Track your hydration and prioritize your health with this monthly water challenge worksheet. Set your goals, monitor your progress, and stay hydrated to feel your best every day.

GOAL

DAY 1

DAY 2

DAY 3

DAY 4

DAY 5

DAY 6

DAY 7

DAY 8

DAY 9

DAY 10

DAY 11

DAY 12

DAY 13

DAY 14

DAY 15

DAY 16

DAY 17

DAY 18

DAY 19

DAY 20

DAY 21

DAY 22

DAY 23

DAY 24

DAY 25

DAY 26

DAY 26

DAY 28

DAY 29

DAY 30

DAY 31

MONTHLY REFLECTIONS

Reflect on your month by acknowledging your wins, addressing challenges, and extracting valuable lessons. Explore how these experiences make you feel and try to capture the essence of the month with one word.

MONTHLY WINS:

....

....

HOW DO YOUR WINS MAKE ME FEEL?

....

....

CHALLENGES:

....

....

HOW CAN I IMPROVE IT?

....

....

TWO LIFE LESSONS I LEARNED THIS MONTH:

....

....

ONE WORD THAT DESCRIBES THIS MONTH:

....

MONTHLY SELF-ASSESSMENT

Use this self-assessment worksheet to evaluate your physical, social, mental, and spiritual well-being. Reflect on your current practices and identify areas for improvement to enhance your overall wellness.

PHYSICAL SELF CARE

	Y	N
Got enough sleep	O	O
Eat healthy	O	O
Balanced diet	O	O
Get regular exercise	O	O
See a healthcare provider when needed	O	O

Note:

MENTAL SELF CARE

	Y	N
Take time to relax	O	O
Joy and fulfillment in activities	O	O
Support system	O	O
Practice mindfulness	O	O
Stay present in the moment	O	O

Note:

SOCIAL SELF CARE

	Y	N
Strong and supportive relationship with friends and family	O	O
Make time for social activity	O	O
Set boundaries	O	O
Say no when necessary	O	O

Note:

SPIRITUAL SELF CARE

	Y	N
Have a sense of purpose and meaning in your life	O	O
Practice self-reflection and mindfulness	O	O
Have a sense of connection to something larger than yourself	O	O

Note:

AFFIRMING MY VALUES

This worksheet will help you clarify your values and priorities by affirming what you are, what you are not, what you will, what you will not, what you can do, what you cannot do, what you want, and what you do not want, in your life.

I AM:	I AM NOT:
I WILL:	**I WILL NOT:**
I CAN:	**I CANNOT:**
I WANT:	**I DO NOT WANT:**

SELF-CARE IN PRACTICE

Explore and enhance your self-care routine with this worksheet. Reflect on relaxation practices, food choices, physical activity, personal connections, and spirituality. Identify any difficulties you may face in these areas. This worksheet will help you prioritize your well-being and develop strategies to overcome challenges.

RELAXATION PRACTICE	DIFFICULT FOR ME
FOOD CHOICES	**DIFFICULT FOR ME**
PHYSICAL ACTIVITY	**DIFFICULT FOR ME**
CONNECTION/SPIRITUALITY	**DIFFICULT FOR ME**

WATER CHALLENGE

Track your hydration and prioritize your health with this monthly water challenge worksheet. Set your goals, monitor your progress, and stay hydrated to feel your best every day.

GOAL

DAY 1 DAY 2 DAY 3 DAY 4

DAY 5 DAY 6 DAY 7 DAY 8

DAY 9 DAY 10 DAY 11 DAY 12

DAY 13 DAY 14 DAY 15 DAY 16

DAY 17 DAY 18 DAY 19 DAY 20

DAY 21 DAY 22 DAY 23 DAY 24

DAY 25 DAY 26 DAY 26 DAY 28

DAY 29 DAY 30 DAY 31

MONTHLY REFLECTIONS

Reflect on your month by acknowledging your wins, addressing challenges, and extracting valuable lessons. Explore how these experiences make you feel and try to capture the essence of the month with one word.

MONTHLY WINS:

....

....

HOW DO YOUR WINS MAKE ME FEEL?

....

....

CHALLENGES:

....

....

HOW CAN I IMPROVE IT?

....

....

TWO LIFE LESSONS I LEARNED THIS MONTH:

....

....

ONE WORD THAT DESCRIBES THIS MONTH:

....

MONTHLY SELF-ASSESSMENT

Use this self-assessment worksheet to evaluate your physical, social, mental, and spiritual well-being. Reflect on your current practices and identify areas for improvement to enhance your overall wellness.

PHYSICAL SELF CARE

	Y	N
Got enough sleep	O	O
Eat healthy	O	O
Balanced diet	O	O
Get regular exercise	O	O
See a healthcare provider when needed	O	O

Note:

MENTAL SELF CARE

	Y	N
Take time to relax	O	O
Joy and fulfillment in activities	O	O
Support system	O	O
Practice mindfulness	O	O
Stay present in the moment	O	O

Note:

SOCIAL SELF CARE

	Y	N
Strong and supportive relationship with friends and family	O	O
Make time for social activity	O	O
Set boundaries	O	O
Say no when necessary	O	O

Note:

SPIRITUAL SELF CARE

	Y	N
Have a sense of purpose and meaning in your life	O	O
Practice self-reflection and mindfulness	O	O
Have a sense of connection to something larger than yourself	O	O

Note:

AFFIRMING MY VALUES

This worksheet will help you clarify your values and priorities by affirming what you are, what you are not, what you will, what you will not, what you can do, what you cannot do, what you want, and what you do not want, in your life.

I AM:	I AM NOT:
I WILL:	I WILL NOT:
I CAN:	I CANNOT:
I WANT:	I DO NOT WANT:

SELF-CARE IN PRACTICE

Explore and enhance your self-care routine with this worksheet. Reflect on relaxation practices, food choices, physical activity, personal connections, and spirituality. Identify any difficulties you may face in these areas. This worksheet will help you prioritize your well-being and develop strategies to overcome challenges.

RELAXATION PRACTICE	DIFFICULT FOR ME
FOOD CHOICES	DIFFICULT FOR ME
PHYSICAL ACTIVITY	DIFFICULT FOR ME
CONNECTION/SPIRITUALITY	DIFFICULT FOR ME

WATER CHALLENGE

Track your hydration and prioritize your health with this monthly water challenge worksheet. Set your goals, monitor your progress, and stay hydrated to feel your best every day.

GOAL

DAY 1

DAY 2

DAY 3

DAY 5

DAY 6

DAY 7

DAY 8

DAY 9

DAY 10

DAY 11

DAY 12

DAY 13

DAY 14

DAY 15

DAY 16

DAY 17

DAY 18

DAY 19

DAY 20

DAY 21

DAY 22

DAY 23

DAY 24

DAY 25

DAY 26

DAY 26

DAY 28

DAY 29

DAY 30

DAY 31

52-WEEK WEIGHT TRACKER

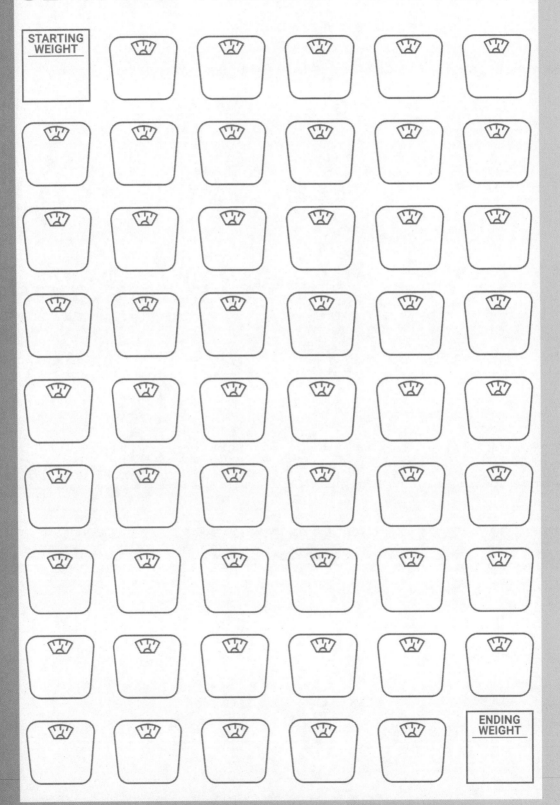

STARTING WEIGHT

ENDING WEIGHT

FREE THOUGHTS

8
MY BALDIE PLAN

With the Baldie Plan, you'll set a path for confidently pursuing your dreams while reclaiming your identity and envisioning a future of limitless possibilities. It's all about setting goals, building resilience, and embracing the uniqueness of your journey.

Through practical strategies and empowering mindset shifts, you'll craft a personalized plan to pursue your aspirations, embrace your baldness with pride, and create a life filled with purpose and fulfillment. So, let's embark on this journey together, shaping the life you've always dreamed of.

MY BALDIE BUCKET LIST

Creating this bucket list can offer clarity of your goals and desires, and help you prioritize what you want to experience or achieve in your life.

Use your Baldie Bucket List to create a road map that explores exciting new experiences, affirms your new freedom and confidence, and that embraces your baldness with joy and empowerment.

☐ ....   ☐ ....

☐ ....   ☐ ....

☐ ....   ☐ ....

☐ ....   ☐ ....

☐ ....   ☐ ....

☐ ....   ☐ ....

☐ ....   ☐ ....

☐ ....   ☐ ....

☐ ....   ☐ ....

☐ ....   ☐ ....

☐ ....   ☐ ....

☐ ....   ☐ ....

☐ ....   ☐ ....

☐ ....   ☐ ....

YEARLY VISION PLANNER

Developing a yearly vision plan helps you set clear and concise goals that embrace your newfound freedom in the year ahead, and that will help you stay focused on what's important for your new path.

Use this planner to confidently set goals and track your progress for personal growth, self-care, and meaningful experiences.

WHAT I WANT MY BALDIE LIFE TO LOOK LIKE THIS YEAR:

....

....

....

....

....

ACTIONS I NEED TO TAKE TO ACHIEVE MY VISION:

☐ .... ☐ ....

☐ .... ☐ ....

☐ .... ☐ ....

☐ .... ☐ ....

☐ .... ☐ ....

☐ .... ☐ ....

☐ .... ☐ ....

☐ .... ☐ ....

DATE: ....

GOALS & DREAMS

Listing your goals and dreams provides clarity on what you want to achieve, keeps you motivated, and helps you stay focused. With professional, personal, and interpersonal goals and dreams defined, you can clearly navigate your new journey with purpose, confidence, and a direction that helps you create a balanced and fulfilling life – a life focused on growth, success, and meaningful connections with others.

PROFESSIONAL GOALS:

1. ....

2. ....

3. ....

4. ....

PERSONAL GOALS:

1. ....

2. ....

3. ....

4. ....

INTERPERSONAL GOALS:

1. ....

2. ....

3. ....

4. ....

DATE: ....

LETTERS TO MYSELF
A LETTER TO MY YOUNGER SELF

Use this worksheet to reflect on your journey and celebrate by writing a letter to your younger self. This letter allows you to address past challenges, celebrate growth, and offer advice with a sense of empathy and understanding for that younger person.

As a baldie, a letter to your younger self about your new freedom, enables you to reflect on your journey, embrace the present, and inspire yourself to live confidently and authentically.

DATE: ....

LETTERS TO MYSELF
A LETTER TO MY CURRENT SELF

Use this worksheet to reflect on your journey and celebrate your present with a letter to your current self.

Share your newfound freedom and empowerment, affirm your resilience and confidence, acknowledge your unique beauty, and offer self encouragement as you navigate your new life with self love, grace and authenticity.

....

....

....

....

....

....

....

....

....

....

....

DATE: ....

LETTERS TO MYSELF
A LETTER TO MY FUTURE SELF

Finally, a letter to your future self allows you to envision the future.
Dare to set intentions, visualize your goals, and inspire yourself to continue
growing and pursuing your dreams with clarity and determination.

In this worksheet, share with your future self of your visions of continued
growth in confidence and empowerment to which you aspire. These
words should motivate yourself to embrace life's adventures with
courage, grace, and authenticity.

DATE: ....

FREE THOUGHTS

9
MY BALDIE LAWS

When you need uplifting and affirmation, turn to the Baldie Laws. Stand firm in these laws and the confidence of all the beautiful women before you – and know you are brave and powerful.

Embrace the wisdom of the Baldie Laws on each day of your journey, drawing strength from the courage of your Baldie sisters. Remember, you are not alone, and you possess the bravery and power to conquer any challenge that comes your way.

MY BALDIE LAW 1

MY LACK OF HAIR NO LONGER CONTROLS MY MOVEMENT.

—SHELIA MARIE HUNTER

MY BALDIE LAW 2

FREEDOM ISN'T ONE SIZE FITS ALL. BALD WIGS OR WRAPS, IT'S YOUR CHOICE.

—SHELIA MARIE HUNTER

MY BALDIE LAW 3

I BREATHE BECAUSE NEW LIFE AWAITS ME.

—SHELIA MARIE HUNTER

MY BALDIE LAW 4

MY VERY PRESENCE IS SOMEONE'S HOPE.

—SHELIA MARIE HUNTER

MY BALDIE LAW 5

ALLOW THE NEW YOU TO BE LOVED.

—SHELIA MARIE HUNTER

MY BALDIE LAW 6

ALWAYS BE YOUR AUTHENTIC SELF. IT'S YOUR SUPERPOWER.

—SHELIA MARIE HUNTER

MY BALDIE LAW 7

FREEDOM COMES WHEN ACCEPTANCE BEGINS.

—SHELIA MARIE HUNTER

MY BALDIE LAW 8

BALD IS MY FREEDOM CHOICE.

—SHELIA MARIE HUNTER

MY BALDIE LAW 9

FREEDOM HAS SHOWN ME TO TREASURE MY TIME.

—SHELIA MARIE HUNTER

MY BALDIE LAW 10

WALKING INTO MY NEW LIFE THAT WAS CREATED FOR ME.

—SHELIA MARIE HUNTER

Baldie Girls

My name is
Shelia Marie Hunter
and I'm SURVIVING
ALOPECIA.

When I woke the morning of March 28,
2018. I had no idea that it would
be my last day in hiding. Never would
I cover My Beautiful Crown again. I felt
so Naked but Free at the same time.
Unsure of what others would think.

My husband and I decided many years
ago about revealing my Alopecia to the
world. But 10 years later my daughter
was finally ok with the world knowing
her mother was Bald. The Shame of
Hair loss affects the entire family.

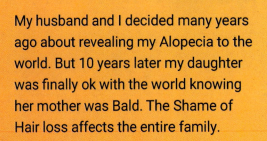

Journal to Freedom

Family First

My quality of life is so much better. No Regret!!!!! I feel Sexier that I ever felt with Hair.

Baldie Girls

Add a photo of you covering. If you
have the photos of the day you
shaved add also.

Share what you felt on that day.
What your family felt.

Tell us your So Free Since date
in the bottom right.

DATE: ....

Journal to Freedom

Add your photos, and photos with
family and friends since you shaved
and living free.

Add your thoughts you've had
since be corning free.

REFLECTIONS

- Remember you are a Baddie, Baldie, and a Boss Lady — the heavens made no mistakes in creating you. You showed so much courage and self-discovery to become FREE. Always remain your authentic self — it's your SUPERPOWER.

- Never let the voices within stifle your dreams – stay resilient. I pray that the journal pages you create bring PEACE, HEALING, AND BRAVERY to share your story fearlessly with others.

- My goal with this journal was for you to find therapy and peace. And I hope that by pouring your heart out on each page, you will one day be liberated and proudly publish your own amazing story.

YOU'RE A BADDIE

YOU'RE A BALDIE

YOU'RE A BOSS LADY

FINAL THOUGHTS

Made in the USA
Columbia, SC
09 August 2024

84a4173c-4df6-495d-b87f-a01fa8ff207aR07